Bugs Rule!

By Kathryn Stevens

The
Child's
World
www.childsworld.com

Published in the United States of America by The Child's World®
1980 Lookout Drive • Mankato, MN 56003-1705
800-599-READ • www.childsworld.com

ACKNOWLEDGMENTS

The Child's World®: Mary Berendes, Publishing Director

Produced by Shoreline Publishing Group LLC
President / Editorial Director: James Buckley, Jr.
Designer: Tom Carling, carlingdesign.com
Cover Design: Slimfilms

Photo Credits
Cover–Dreamstime.com
Interior–Corbis: 19, 23, 26; Dreamstime.com: 6, 7, 9, 12, 15, 16, 18, 20, 21, 24, 29; iStock: 5, 10, 12, 25, 27, 28.

LIBRARY OF CONGRESS CATALOG-IN-PUBLICATION DATA

Stevens, Kathryn, 1954–.
  Bugs rule! / by Kathryn Stevens.
      p. cm. — (Reading rocks!)
  Includes index.
  ISBN-13: 978-1-59296-856-5 (library bound : alk. paper)
  ISBN-10: 1-59296-856-2 (library bound : alk. paper)
  1. Insects—Juvenile literature 2. Insect pests—Juvenile literature I. Title. II. Series.

  QL467.2.S776 2007
  595.7—dc22

                                    2007004200

CONTENTS

SMALL BUT

Amazing

Big is bad, right? Don't be too sure. Bugs aren't very big compared to you or me. But for their size, they're some of the toughest animals around!

But what exactly are "bugs"? People use this word to mean all kinds of creepy-crawlers. Mostly they use it to mean six-legged **insects**. Sometimes they use it for spiders, mites, and ticks—which are actually eight-legged **arachnids**. Sometimes they use it for many-legged centipedes and millipedes. Scientists call all these creepy-crawlers by their

proper names. They use the word "bugs" only for certain kinds of "true bugs." True bugs have mouthparts made for sucking. Adults have two pairs of different wings. Scientists believe that there are between 35,000 and 50,000 kinds of true bugs.

This stink bug is a great example of a "true bug."

Scientists have identified more than a million different kinds of insects. There are more insects on Earth than all other animals put together.

Here's a good look at the six skinny legs of a walkingstick.

The biggest bug of all time was a dragonfly that lived 250 million years ago. It had a wingspan of over two feet (61 cm).

Bugs have lots of different ways of moving. Some of them fly. Others crawl, swim, or dig holes underground. They eat lots of different foods, too. Many bugs eat only plants. But some eat animal foods—and some of these bugs are hunters and killers.

Bugs come in all sizes and shapes. How big can they get? Pretty big! One Malaysian walkingstick was measured at almost 22 inches (over 55 centimeters) long. The white witch moth of South America has a **wingspan** of 11 inches (28 cm).

Spiders can get big, too. Tarantulas are the biggest. There are lots of different kinds of tarantulas. The largest are goliath bird-eating spiders. These South American giants can be as much as 11 inches (28 cm) across. That's as big as a dinner plate!

What's for Dinner?

Some bugs eat things we think are pretty disgusting. Maggots are fly **larvae**, before they turn into adults. What do they eat? Dead animals and other rotting food— and even rotting flesh on live animals! Dung beetles eat something else that seems disgusting—animal poop.

The white blobs on this hornworm are actually tiny wasp eggs.

Other bugs, though, are very small. Fairyflies are tiny insects that lay eggs inside other insects' eggs. They're only eight-thousands of an inch (one-fifth of a millimeter) long. Some kinds of adult wasps are even smaller. The males of one kind measure a little over five thousands of an inch (139 millionths of a meter). That's not much bigger than the width of a human hair.

Some bugs are amazing athletes for their size. You've probably seen how far a grasshopper can jump. Fleas are much smaller, but they're even better at jumping. Most fleas are less than an eighth of an inch (3 mm) long. But the tiny common flea can jump 200 times its own body length. What does that mean in human terms? Say you're 54 inches (137 cm) tall. You'd be able to jump 900 feet (274 m)!

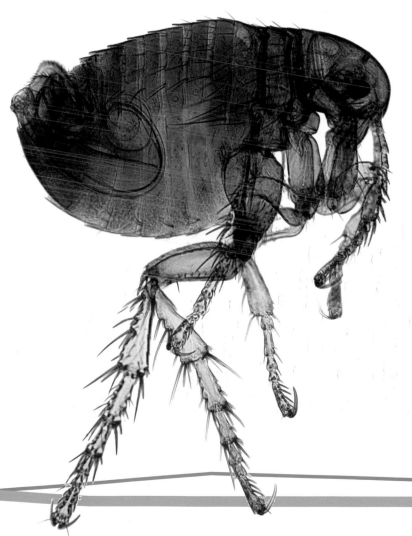

Check out the long, powerful legs in this closeup flea photo.

For their size, some bugs are really fast, too. It's hard to measure exactly how fast bugs can fly. Scientists are working on it, though. They've timed desert locusts flying almost 21 miles (34 km) per hour. Some bugs don't fly that fast, but they work pretty hard at it. One kind of tiny midge flaps its wings over a thousand times every second.

Here's a close-up look at the speedy locust.

And some bugs run pretty fast—especially for their size. The fastest is the Australian tiger beetle, which can run over 8 feet (2.5 m) in one second.

A tiny ant is strong enough to carry a leaf that is much bigger than the ant's body.

Some bugs are really strong. For their size, ants are one of the strongest. They can pull 50 times their body weight. Say you weigh 70 pounds (32 kg). Can you pull 3,500 pounds (1,588 kg)? That's as heavy as a car or a small pickup truck. You could pull it easily if you were as strong as an ant!

Some bugs make their own light! The bodies of fireflies make chemicals that glow. The fireflies blink their lights to "talk" to each other.

When people or animals are social, they live together and help each other.

Many bugs live alone, but some live in groups. Some **social** insects such as ants, bees, and termites live in big groups. Each group is called a **colony**. Every insect in a colony has a job to do.

Termite colonies can be huge. In Africa and Australia, some colonies have three million termites. These termites build big mounds for their homes. The tallest termite mound ever measured was in Africa. It was 42 feet (almost 13 m) tall! That's as tall as a four-story building.

How long do bugs live? Many don't live very long. In fact, some mayflies live for less than 24 hours! But some bugs live much longer. Some queen ants live for almost 30 years. Pet tarantulas sometimes live that long, too. Some termite queens might live to be 50 years old. And all that time, they're laying 6,000 to 7,000 eggs every day.

Tarantulas can be good pets, as long as you handle them carefully.

BUGS THAT CAN Kill

Some bugs hunt and kill other animals for food. These **predators** have all sorts of ways of catching their **prey**. Some are flying killers. Dragonflies fly so well, they can catch their prey in mid-air! Some killer bugs do their hunting in the water. Giant water bugs live in the water and have a nasty bite. Some of these insects are over 4 inches (10 cm) long. They eat small animals such as fish, snails, and even frogs. Other killer bugs hunt on the ground, on plants, and in lots of other places. Spiders are one of the most common. Everybody has seen these killers and their prey. Many spiders spin sticky webs that catch other bugs. Other spiders jump on their prey instead. Spiders make **venom** that they shoot into their prey. The venom poisons the prey and breaks down the animal's insides. That makes it easier for the spider to eat.

Spitting spiders spit out sticky, poisonous silk to catch their prey.

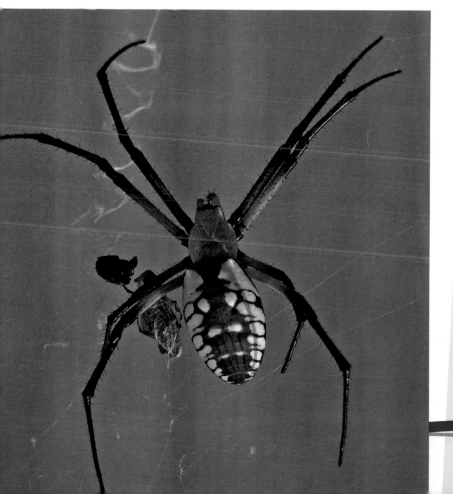

This wasp spider has wrapped up an insect and is preparing to make it into a meal.

The name "centipede" means "100 feet." However, most centipedes don't have quite that many.

Centipedes are hunters with dozens of legs—many more than you find on insects or spiders. They also have poisonous claws just behind their heads. Centipedes go into all sorts of places looking for prey. You've probably seen them in your basement, or under rocks you've

turned over. Most North American centipedes are fairly small. But giant centipedes that live in South America are over 10 inches (25 cm) long! Big centipedes like these can hunt larger prey than bugs. They hunt lizards, snakes, frogs, mice, and other small animals.

Another type of animal has lots of legs—but lots of bodies, too. Army ants are killer insects that hunt in big groups. These ants live in many parts of the world. Most other kinds of ants stay in one place and build nests. But enormous army-ant colonies travel from place to place. As they travel, they attack and kill any bugs and small animals they find in their path.

Millipedes look like centipedes, but they're very different animals. They have rounder bodies and shorter legs, and they're not hunters. Instead, millipedes eat dead plant and animal matter.

Small But Dangerous

What do you think are the most dangerous bugs in the world? Spiders? Killer bees? Wasps? Nope! They're mosquitoes. These little blood suckers carry some deadly diseases, including **malaria**. Mosquitoes can spread this disease when they bite people. Every year, some 500 million people get malaria. Over 1 million of them die—most of them young children in Africa.

Some bugs don't kill their prey before they eat it. Instead, they eat it alive! Tarantula hawks are big wasps—some are almost 4 inches (10 cm) long. They lay their eggs on tarantula spiders. The wasp's sting makes the spider unable to move. When the eggs hatch, the wasp larvae eat the helpless spider.

Some bugs don't kill their dinner at all. Instead, they live off the animal while it's alive. Animals that feed off a living host are called **parasites**. Lots of parasites suck blood. Sometimes parasites carry diseases that can make their hosts get sick or even die.

The tarantula hawk wasp is the last thing a tarantula wants to see buzzing around.

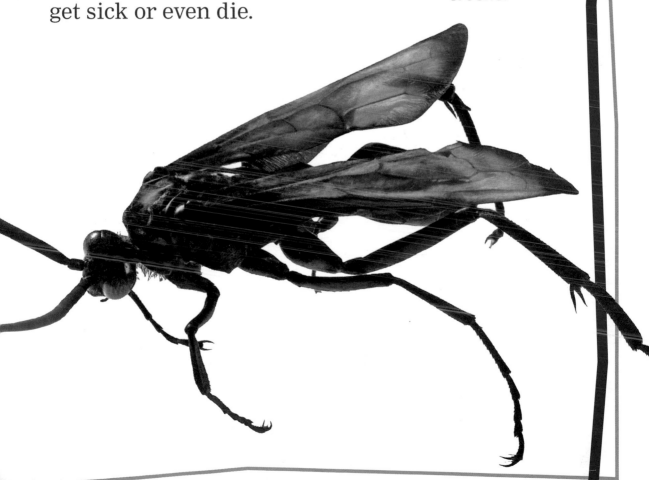

Bees live in tightly packed colonies. Some scientists think that bees identify each other by smell.

Bugs don't hunt and kill people for food—we're too big! But some bugs can kill people by accident. When wasps or bees sting, they're only trying to protect themselves or their nests. For most people the stings just hurt for a moment. But some people are **allergic** to the stings. They can get sick or even die. People who are allergic to stings often carry special medicine with them. If they are stung, they take this medicine right away to help avoid getting sick.

Killer bees live in some warm areas of the world. When they get upset, they attack and sting in large groups. Killer bees are not as common as news stories make them seem.

You can tell a wasp by the yellow marks near its head and middle.

3

BUGS THAT BUG

People

Some bugs just won't leave people alone. They're the bugs we think of as real pests. Some of them bite, sting, or suck blood. Some carry germs. Lots of them live in people's homes. Others are more of a problem outside. But all of these pests are ones that people dislike.

Did you know that some bugs actually live in your skin? Tiny mites live way down at the bottom of people's hairs. They're only about one-hundredth of an inch (less than three-hundredths of a centimeter) long. You don't even know they're there!

Tiny head lice live in people's hair and suck their blood. Kids sometimes catch head lice at school. Even the cleanest kids can get them. Getting rid of these parasites is difficult, but it's important.

This scientist is looking at a blow-up view of a louse. Lice is the word for more than one louse.

Mosquitoes lay their eggs around water. They're so light, they can rest on the surface of the water!

Some other bugs suck people's blood, too. Besides carrying diseases, mosquitoes can be real pests. Only female mosquitoes bite. On hot summer nights they buzz and swarm around you. Their bites itch like mad!

Some kinds of ticks also suck people's blood. These eight-legged pests live outdoors. Some of them are so tiny that they're hard to see. They wait for a blood-filled animal to come walking by. They hook on, then find a quiet spot. They make a hole in the animal's skin, then drink their fill—of blood!

Some ticks carry diseases, too. In North America, deer ticks carry Lyme disease.

Some types of flies are also blood suckers. Horseflies and deerflies are common summertime pests in North America. The males eat plant juices, but the females suck blood. They bite to make a small hole in the skin, then drink the blood.

You'll never see a tick this big! Ticks are actually smaller than this letter "e."

Too Small to See

Some bugs live off parts of yourself that you leave behind. We all shed tiny scales of skin—lots of them. Dust mites love to eat those scales. These little eight-legged bugs are everywhere. They live in your mattresses, blankets, and rugs. Most people never notice them. But some people are allergic to dust mites.

Bedbugs are blood-suckers that feed on people who are sleeping. They're a real problem in some places. These flat, brown insects are about the size of an apple seed. They live in beds, rugs, and furniture. Bedbugs are active at night—especially about an hour before dawn. They seek out warm bodies and people's breath. Their bites can be itchy and red.

Bedbugs were almost gone from North America. Now they're starting to reappear, especially in hotels and motels.

Some bugs don't bite, but we think of them as pests when they invade our homes. Ants are sometimes a problem in people's homes. So are cockroaches. Cockroaches come out at night and eat any food they can find. Getting rid of cockroaches isn't easy! They hide well, and they're really tough. Flies can be a nuisance, too. How many times have you had to shoo them away from a picnic table? Keeping things clean makes our homes less appealing to these pests.

Cockroaches can be hard to kill. A cockroach can live for several days even if it loses its head!

Cockroaches use their long antennae to search for food.

Most kinds of ants aren't dangerous. Some kinds, though, have painful bites or stings. They include fire ants, army ants, driver ants, and Australian bulldog ants. If something threatens these types of ant colonies, the ants attack, stinging and biting viciously.

Fleas can be pests, too. They suck animals' blood and can spread diseases. Different kinds bite different kinds of animals, including cats and dogs—and people. Years ago, fleas were a big problem. They helped spread a deadly disease called plague (PLAYG). Millions of people died of plague. Entire cities were wiped out. Fleas are still a problem in some parts of the world.

Bugs are an important part of the natural world. Many of them are a help to us. For instance, bees help flowers grow by carrying **pollen**. Some bugs are pests, though, and we do our best to deal with them. Helpers or pests, insects are all part of life on our big, colorful planet!

In their travels from flower to flower, bees spread pollen. Pollen helps flowers grow.

GLOSSARY

allergic   having a bad physical reaction to something

arachnids   boneless animals with eight legs, two main body parts, and no wings.

colony   a group of animals of the same kind that live together

insects   boneless animals that have six legs, three main body parts, and usually one or two pairs of wings

larvae   young, wingless, often wormlike forms of some insects when they first hatch from their eggs.

malaria   a blood disease spread by mosquitoes

parasite   a plant or animal that lives on or inside other living things, feeding off of them

pollen   a powder in plants that helps produce seeds

predators   animals that hunt and kill other animals for food

prey   animals that other animals hunt as food

social   wanting to be with others of one's own kind

venom   a poisonous substance that some animals produce and use to harm other animals, usually by biting or stinging

wingspan   the distance from one wing tip to the other in a pair of wings

FIND OUT MORE

BOOKS

Amazing Bugs
> *By Miranda MacQuitty.* (DK Publishing, 1996)
> Drawings and photos of the inside of different bugs highlight this informative book.

The Best Book of Bugs
> *By Claire Llewellyn.* (Kingfisher, 1998)
> See even more great pictures of bugs, and learn many more cool facts in this big book.

Bugs: Eyewonder
> *By Penelope York.* (DK Publishing, 2002)
> This book features lots of close-up photos of bugs and their body parts.

Starting with Nature Bug Book
> *By Pamela Hickman.* (Kids Can Press, 2001)
> This bug-filled book includes experiments you can try to learn more about crawling things.

WEB SITES

Visit our Web page for lots of links about bugs:
> www.childsworld.com/links

Note to Parents, Teachers, and Librarians: We routinely check our Web links to make sure they're safe, active sites—so encourage your readers to check them out!

INDEX

KATHRYN STEVENS is an archaeologist as well as an editor and author of numerous children's books on nature and science, geography, and other topics. She lives in western Wisconsin, where she spends her spare time enjoying the outdoors, restoring a Victorian house, and making pet-therapy visits with her dog.